Also by Rosamond S. King
Rock | Salt | Stone
Island Bodies: Transgressive Sexualities in the Caribbean Imagination
At My Belly & My Back

See www.rosamondSking.black for the *All the Rage* "v-book" – video
performances of selected poems.

ALL THE RAGE

By Rosamond S. King

Nightboat Books
New York

Copyright © 2021 by Rosamond S. King
All rights reserved
Printed in the United States

ISBN: 978-1-64362-071-8

Design & typesetting by Astryd Design Inc.
Text set in Adobe Caslon Pro and Avenir

Cataloging-in-publication data is available from the Library of Congress

Nightboat Books
New York
www.nightboat.org

for Mama Rosa
who was quiet
and
for Pepper King
who was loud

!

Welcome to the Abattoir

Avant–Garde Is a Term of War

Blood Is the New Hot Sauce

For the Women

That Would Be Telling

Double Valence

Sunshine Sigh

This book / is for you
whether or not you survived

...

This book is for you
sleeping with the light on so
your eyes will open to brightness
no matter the weather

...

This book is for
you, whether you quarantine
stuffing your face
or (and) reorganizing drawers
streaming
staring

...

This book is
for you

and the women who told me
the world
does not need
these poems

Welcome to the Abattoir

I do not want to be a monster
. I do not want to be a cat
. If I want to be a sexy nurse or valet
It will not be in public, where
My mask is used daily
. When it's off, the gaze
Sees caricature
In my skin
. Tell me
What is it like to want
To be a monster
?

America the beautiful

I am not safe – and neither are you

Everything big and abundant. If it's more beautiful Elsewhere, it's
shinier here. Anything bad is better than the alternative
:
Say it with me:
                           ə
                           buh
no   ah - buh
yes
        –

We live in the most *gorgeous* abattoir
(from the French, but better here
. Like french fries, which make us round and marbled
. Our vegetables covered with cheese, our fruits glazed with glycerin
into glossiness
– *Welcome to the Abattoir*

.

Elsewhere, the abattoir is hidden
; the blood drained away. Here, whole neighborhoods are abattoirs
. True
, some never make it out, but while they're here, we
distract them with baubled accessories and bubbled beverages

Etymology of a Scream

Lily does not social distance
Anthurium won't mask
stubborn, defiant, they grab
dark loam and reach for bright
.

It took too many years to understand
the soil soaked, bloodied
before before New Netherlanders'
footsteps. Today, wishing for Anthurium
watching Lily, notice Bedstraw
not an apparition, Turtlehead
, and notice the tree. Shagbark is angry
and the soil moans, not for the darks who
won't call themselves Garifuna anymore – not for
the lights replacing them without claiming anyone
, nor the lights that came before, who loved the
land deeply, inserting wayfaring roses and sauce-bound
tomatoes, who could not hear any moans
not from Calàbbria or Sicily or
. So long the soil's keening, the tree thunders
for the Canarsee, for the Nyack, for so long
inaudible to most, and assumed
doomed, like everything else, to belong to the few who
could hear it. Some said Questo è
mio, others Jesteś moja or Ent I paid for dis? Is we time now
. None of us hearing beyond our own
lament, none acknowledging our cousins
Nyack, Canarsee, Lenaape, Ashinaabe
mourning with screaming wails not

because they were first to walk
here, not because theirs was the first
blood the ground was forced to drink
, but because they are still here
and we could together feel the beating
heart of the earth, embrace
the trees' knowledge, their ability
to smile. The ground wails
. The Shagbark thunders, because
we do not know our cousins, not
their language, their knowledge – not
even their names. Worse, those who
acknowledge and think all our kin
are dead
   . Mourn those who came
before and the absence among those who
remain, and that we, uninvited guests
, will not name Lenaape, Canarsee
, Nyack, Honeoye, Turtlehead, Shagbark, Bedstraw
 and will call none of them family

sometime in the near future
we drown in the distinct past
grinning, it grabs the
shirt of the skittish present
while someone beats us senseless

in the daze, forward
and backward get confused

All of us are born in blood
but those born in the Abattoir
smell it every day – a
reminder that our death
is imminent and will be swift
and bloody
.

Elsewhere, childhood is different
bloodied only by scrapes and falls. Elsewhere
People are free of the smell of iron in their own hair
, sweat, clothes. They are
free of the taste of it

.

If you're just walking through, you mightn't notice the ooze
. But cartwheeling in the Abattoir, our palms will be printed
with it, our footballs and soccer balls and dodge
balls slick with blood, and we realize our home
is a zoo for the underprivileged and People
, Elsewhere People will visit and pet us with one well-meaning hand
while holding nosegays with the other. We realize at five or seven or
nine that we are not meant to ever leave, that we live surrounded
by blood and killing machines because
we are meant to die young. Our six or eight or nine
yearold selves watch Elsewhere wipe their feet on the way out

It's called the Abattoir because we live under
the blade. It's called the Abattoir because
there is a larger economy based on our
systematic, continuous
and premature death
. It is the outside inside
a part of and separate

.

Yonder they do love our
flesh; they love it jiggling
they love it naked they
love. it. sweating
. They love it
kneeling or prone
grinning
or weeping, preferably
all at the same time

and with feeling

or
You Betta Re Cog Nize
for and from A. Marquez

ball
boys
Bronx
sweat
shirts
eso
shoes not Jordans
want to be
boys
no te preocupe
hombre
Bronx ballin
don't sweat it

Blue shirt
voices drop
blunt knowledge
allyouniggersgetupagainstthewall
Puerto Ricans stand
center court
bounce   bounce   till
daytime nightstick
All. You. Niggers. Upagainst. Thewall
!
Boricua Bronx
brown black boys
if you
didn't
know
now

13

Independence from Treaties

Now that treaties are being read
not eaten (breakfast of champions
), now we are beyond the worth
of words on paper, a signature
and an X, details of value
, worth, own her ship, belonging. Now
independence is declared from treaties
, now tragedy recorded
on paper, in pixels
. After *this* tragedy, eat your treaties
see what champions
are bound by

21st Century Goddamn

Everybody knows about Baltimore
Everybody knows about Staten Island
Everybody knows about Cleveland
about Texas
? about Chicago
Everybody knows about skittles
Everybody knows that if   I die in police custody
I did   not   commit suicide
EVERYBODY knows about Ferguson
Who knows about the 129th Corps Support Battalion, about DC,
about Tallahassee, Rantoul, Tulsa, Plymouth, Plantation – yeah,
Plantation, Florida
– Everybody knows
not every body
gets out of this alive

The Known and Unknown

The known dead do not need
to be ghosts, honored and invoked
as they are. The ignored
, forgotten, unknown – their smile
unremembered, their rose vines
ripped away, *they* will never leave

for La Table Ronde

This is how Elsewhere People event
: Summon us to an address
. Order us not to disclose name
or occupation, neglect to mention
the place's inaccessibility or
the large, aggressive dog
. Do nothing
when the dog proceeds
to chew one of your "guest's" pants
. This is how things are done Elsewhere
: there is no table, there is no
dinner. Pictures of mutilated dark bodies
line the walls, but fewer Blacks are
on the bookshelves, and fewer still present
at their round "table," at their "dinner
"party with the same old
talking heads
—

This is how they do things
.: Afterwards, offering snacks from
the same unwashed hand that fed the dog

Avant–Garde Is a Term of War

Breathe. As in
            to take a breath
. Synonym for breath: respiration
.

Can't. As in unable to

.

I. As in first person singular
. Homonym for I: eye

.

Everyone knows who the I is – who are we
? How big are your eyes – whose suffocation are you able to see
                    violence against trans people (also) spectacular
            . as in a spectacle, often resulting in rape, other grievous
                                    injury, or death
                            . But the I can't see
                . police, state violence against women, especially
                    poor women of color, so normalized it is
                            typically invisible to the I

.

can't breathe ≠ lack of respiration
respite = respiration
aspiration: not loosening the noose
                                    but its removal
!   *chokehold bans =*
                please find another way to kill Black people
        body cameras = please press record when you kill Black people
repealed privacy laws = the number of Black people you've killed must be
                                    made public

.

Aspiration

(?)(!):

DISINVEST

Revitalization (from vīta, Latin for life) of communities, beginning with

clean water, schools

accessible routes to legal, living-wage jobs

. Dismantling   structures of underdevelopment

economic, political, and legal

work by white people, among white people

I/we/you should not act

like the only right we have is

to remain silent

. Breathe. As in

:

Avant–Garde
Is a Term of War

The safety is off
! we have to laugh
(safety's always off
war begins at home
DV: we are the calvalry
even in war
laughter
lip licking
even in war
fried dough pepper
dished we are
calvalry we
avant-garde front line
troops facing down
torches shots spit
tossed coffee
we the avant guard
taking direct hits
& we the
calvary wounds salved
w/ unsalted butter
hate sucked & spit
out by the same mouth
reminding us
: our skin is velvet
we gorgeous
not hidden
not buried

for Jayne

A banana is not a gun[*]
a wallet[†] is a gun
, a phone[¥] is a gun
, a vegetable peeler[§] is
a deadly knife
. What do you have
holstered

[*] Josephine Baker
[†] Amadou Diallo
[¥] Stephon Alonzo Clark
[§] Bích Câu Thi Trân

Breathe
. As in what if
the shadow is gold
en? Breathe. As in
hale assuming
exhale. Imagine
that.   As in first
person singular. Homonym
: 👁 . As in subject. As
in centeroftheworld as in
mundane. The opposite of spectacle
spectacular. This is just us
breathing. Imagine
normalized respite
gold in shadows
. You have the
right to breathe and remain
. Imagine
that

.

golden breath
slippering away
mundane. you
imagine the equator
both edge and center
of the world. precipice
. imagine spectacular
get spectacle
d. why is second person
plural addressed to first
person singular
: "you people
"? prepositions describe
an object or person
's relation to
another object
or
what happens when
one
third person singular
or plural, not royal
dangles

[untitled] **

trump – meanings: winner (n), outdo (v
)winner (n) – meaning: victor (n
)victor synonyms: champion (n); champ (n); conqueror
         (n); front-runner (n); leader (n); first past the post (n
)victor antonyms: dark horse (n), loser (n
)winner (n) – meaning: success (n
)success synonyms: hit (n or v), star (n), cert (n), sensation
         (pos. or neg.), triumph (n), brilliant idea (n), sure thing (n
)success antonyms: dark horse (n), failure (n
)outdo (v) – meaning: exceed (v
)outdo synonyms: undermine (v), outmaneuver (v), outplay (v),
go one better (v), call somebody's bluff (v), catch somebody napping
         (v), steal a march on somebody (v
)success antonyms: dark horse (n), failure (n
)
trump synonyms: winner (n), decider (n), trump card (n
)decider (n) – meaning: game (n
)game synonyms: match (n or v), contest (n or v), trial (n), playoff
(n
), shoot-out (n), tie-break (n
)trump card (n) – meaning (1): a card from the suit that has been
      chosen as the most valuable for a particular card game
   trump card (n) – meaning (2): something that gives someone an
   advantage
      trump card synonyms: race card (n), race & class card (n
)outsider card (n), never-saw-it-coming (v
)

**With thanks and apologies to Microsoft® Word for Mac 2011, Version 14.6.9 (160926) & merriam–webster.com

we are compliant
: biting down hard until teeth crack
: taking all the dispensed medication
we are silent when you grope us
; we are a good fit; we never question
we are good Americans; we eat everything on our plate

Bandin belly in Brooklyn
Bandin belly in Ferguson
Bandin belly in Port-au-Prince
in
in
in a man in uniform
an unarmed woman
an unarmed man
an unarmed child

BAWL! Bawl and bandyubelly
!
always a bawl is a bawl is a bawl

what is a 21st century belly band
?
how we can ban belly beyond the Abattoir
? is the 21st century – we still
suckin salt? time
to spit it back
all that mouth water, all that
eye water, leh we
stream it back to de source
we want to fire de work of
sufferation
but we can't when we always
planning funerals

– instead, leh we
fire de armed occupation
(dem cyan kill all of we
dem need us still, an underclass
to support the entire architecture. leh we
dismantle de machines into pieces

How do we bear it
?
We put our tongue between
our teeth. If necessary
we swallow protein

.

your safe ardor
– ally the noun
not the action
self-satisfied
likes & retwittering
– your safe arbor
thorn full on
the other hand
on the other

whose coagulation
pools below? don't
worry
: your safe parlor
your safe larder await
. the flood is outside
your door

"yonder they do not
love your flesh

Elsewhere
they do not love our flesh
they Elsewhere
they do not
love our flesh
Elsewhere
they do not love

our flesh
under them
do not love

on love
:
love our flesh
love under our flesh
do not not love

do not love on their
Elsewhere flesh

they love
. they do not love
our flesh

do not
do nothing

Elsewhere
they do not have our flesh

love

.

** from *Beloved* by Toni Morrison

Blood Is the New Hot Sauce

sweet salt
　bitter
sour their
umami is
blood, ours

blood is the new hot sauce
, bottled condiment
sold behind glass at Whole
Paycheck, served
with tiny spoons by
request at exclusive tasting
menu joints named after
tools or the least-known
cuts of meat

knew it was coming
after fish head and ox tail
once thought trash for im
migrants, now served haute

knew it was coming after
bone marrow and brains

Gentrifying the Abattoir

Steel eats the Abattoir because
It tastes good
. There is no meat without slaughter
, No rare sear without blood
. Every meal could use a little
Salt, a little music, a dot of color
. Stealers
Eating the Abattoir
Because we taste good

.

Abattoir Gentrification

When someone's son becomes a meat
offering on our block, they
hire one of us to scrub the blood
away – can understand that

but they've been scrubbing us away
painting over bronzed cherubs

even the tomatoes Italians planted
before they turned white uprooted
, their coagulated roses trimmed
into respectable fence

as if
no thing happened here. They get
to twenty-first century homestead, pilgrim
, pogrom, genocide

our dead are ghosts

though we were ghosts to them before
dying

they will say nothing
to their children and when
they are petulantly rebellious, parents
will say nothing of note happened here
before you
insist they never knew what makes prime rare

.

The agent winks she's putting the Abba
in Abattoir": others say "Aba-T" is
where "the noir's all gone
"! ☺
When blood sullies their planters of
greenery while someone's son's mother
and a well-practiced coterie bawl too
loud and too long, they call the
to be protected from, from

after our sweet meat
comes blood
with mustard tang
clotted into curds or
drizzled fresh onto ice
cream, fruit, smeared & left
to dry, decorating a half
empty plate. flaked like bonito
a subtle earthiness
not always identifiable

you knew
it was
we were
coming after

Oops

!
Careful we have to be
: Opening the door
, Getting our wallets
, Playing in a park
, Switching lanes
, Sitting in our own home
, Standing in our own backyard
, Sleeping in our own bed
Can be fatal
. Oops
! Ask? There is no ask
. Try? There is no try
. There is only shoot
And strangle
. Oops
! Accidental slaughter
Is an epidemic
In the Abattoir
And on the Rez

.

No
, Sir
, Nobody shot me
. We just
Sweat blood
Naturally

.

No sun today
. Rain seems not
tears, but retribution
. All of us are victims
, none of us are pure
; none of us are safe
. Things are bad, and we
will not be comforted
. We'd rather re-watch
the tragedy, re-tell our
horrors, spew
about revenge
. We don't want comfort
yet – we want vindication
, acknowledgement
, the nodding of heads saying
yes, this happened, and
it   is   horrible. No
comfort, not yet – we want
the mirror of our blood
and fear and agony on
another face. We have
forgotten comfort, how
and where to look for it

(after depart meant

Blind-colored glasses and the damocles is in
Visible. No threat against an Abattoir dweller enrages
Elsewhere. Even the shock of murder lasts only
One news cycle. Rinse and repeat. But
Care covers Elsewhere women
Like a dropped cloth   Like a tablecloth
Protecting precious   The straight, pressed
From blood spatter   Foundation of every wholesome
.

Finish your food – don't you know
Child run in the Abattoir
Are starving? But don't clean your plate
; Lucy here is happy to have that job
.

Blind-colored classes and
The damocles is in\visible over
The Abattoir
Over Elsewhere too

For the Women

Some of us
did not
die

.

What we live
we would not wish
on anyone

.

what   in danger
meant   when her
door was   broken down by in
truders with guns   what
in danger meant
: the system is not broken
the system   is not mal
functioning
; the system   does not
    have   a   glitch
– the system is working as
intended. the system
is working
exactly as intended

A Judge Supreme

He couldn't help
himself and so he helped himself
cop   a feel   here
steal a kiss   there
and no one said any
thing that could be heard   nothing
happened   to him
so he helped him   self
some more. a second
helping. and a third   again
again   part of the training
to judge

    What People say is false
that there is no one to stop him
now. there is always someone
as long as those men
  need domin on
               i
there is someone
as long as there is cut
glass – the large one, for
grooming, and the ones
making not as they
appear   :history

                i.e
him in the rear
view, him is that me
? distorted, no, not
that is me!? as long as
·//   yes
there is
someone who might

This is for the women

Holds a gun like a claw
It would tear out our humanity if
it thought we had any
Holds a badge like a claw
to make our dignity bleed
to make us gag
this claw digs its blunt
into us – *swallow it*
or else
.

The badge tells us to get
naked and like it
flashlight pricks our belly
then asphalt grinds our knees
gun tells you to like it
so we like it better than prison
better than more flashlights more
badges more guns
.

Laughter, like a claw
that never leaves us never removes
its pointy end from our
throat now stretched wide
a claw to suck the flesh off of

and our whole body
is our throat stretched
wide am I still screaming why
am I still screaming a receptacle
doesn't scream a waste bin doesn't
scream a throat filled with a claw
shouldn't be able to

.

A throat that is a whole body
resonates at an other frequency
sometimes in our everyday we feel
the earth thrumming with
the scream of a throat that is
a body that a claw tried to fill
and failed tried to fill and failed
the throat that is a body pierced
by the thing like a claw screams
and bleeds and the blood dries
but the scream goes on forever
. It does not become a song
– but there is a song. The pierced hole
is a second throat a doubled
sound scream is thrumming ground

song is ringing ears hear
? Hear! *Here*
!

For the women assaulted and raped by former Oklahoma City Police Officer D——l H————
—w, who targeted Black women for his crimes because he believed if they told, no one would
believe them.

54

For the policeman who wept as he was convicted of raping and sexually assaulting more than a dozen Black women

There is no suicide for you
and not only because other blue boys
collect checks to keep you alive
– should you die in custody, we'll believe
it was the spirit of Sandra Bland who
choked you with her own two hands, or
LaVena Johnson, who knows
a thing or two about getting shot with your own gun
. Watch, suicide
. Now that your sadism, your power
are no longer available. Watch
and wait; watch suicide: learn
your own deadly lessons

.

Numbers

7 months of terror
on the force
that we know of

13 women reported
13 women that we know of
ages 17 to 57
2 women suing, civilly

he was 29 years old
he got 263 years of jail
after being tried with 36 counts

Sexual battery – Guilty – eight years
Procuring lewd exhibition – Not guilty
Burglary – Not guilty
Procuring lewd exhibition – Guilty – five years
Procuring lewd exhibition – Guilty – five years
Stalking – Not guilty
Sexual battery – Not guilty
Forcible oral sodomy – Guilty – 20 years
First-degree rape – Not guilty
Forcible oral sodomy – Guilty – 16 years
First-degree rape – Guilty – 30 years
Forcible oral sodomy – Not guilty
Sexual battery – Guilty – eight years
Sexual battery – Guilty – eight years
Procuring lewd exhibition – Guilty – five years
Forcible oral sodomy – Guilty – 16 years
Forcible oral sodomy – Not guilty

Procuring lewd exhibition – Not guilty
Procuring lewd exhibition – Not guilty
First-degree rape – Not guilty
Sexual battery – Not guilty
Sexual battery – Not guilty
Sexual battery – Not guilty
Forcible oral sodomy – Not guilty
Second-degree rape – Not guilty
Indecent exposure – Not guilty
Forcible oral sodomy – Guilty – 16 years
First-degree rape – Guilty – 30 years
First-degree rape – Guilty – 30 years
Sexual battery – Guilty – eight years
Second-degree rape – Guilty – 12 years
First-degree rape – Guilty – 30 years
Sexual battery – Guilty – eight years
Sexual battery – Guilty – eight years
Procuring lewd exhibition – Not guilty
Procuring lewd exhibition – Not guilty*
how often is not guilty not innocent

263 years
3,428 menstrual cycles
give or take

263 years

credit for time served

sentences to be served concurrently

  * from "Holtzclaw found guilty of 18 counts in sexual assault case" by Zak Patterson, 10:24 PM CST Dec 10, 2015 accessed 24 April 2016 http://www.koco.com/news/verdict-reached-in-sexual-assault-case-of-former-okc-police-officer/36837162

| BLDM   /   BLM |

BLDM	BLM
Bend Lives to Malt Track	Blame Lite Tracks
Team Trivot Lacks Blend	TBT Cave Marks Lie
Lve, Tame Black Riots	Black Treacle Mist V
Black Team Nt Loved, Stir	Mr. Believe Salt Tack
Dream, Tab, Live Tons, Lckt	Black Matters Live
MLK Don't Taste Crib Veal	Black Matters: Live!
Bedlam Natter Lit Sock	Black LiveStream
Ntl Bad Lovesick Matter	Blacks, Live Matter
Matter, Black Lives Don't	Live Blacks Matter

Not Just Another
Dead Black Man

who buried you
? who was last
at the edge
after wet clods
on wood silenced
, became earth and earth
? who keened, who cried
ugly, wailed the traditional
way. for all of us

we make conspiracy over our dead
wailing demands and grief
hashtagging our rage but not
blueprints, not plans. chaff
is free; pulp is sold by the
quarter pound

REPARATIONS 2

Yu won't speak truth
, say time passed past
fuh reconciliation. So
leh we talk retribution
:

That Would Be Telling

"We've got white people
."Yes we do
."We've got white people
."How 'bout you
?

We hold these truths against you
You hold these truths as self-defense
    :   15 feet away self-defense
    :   uniformed gun vs unarmed civilian self-defense
    :   how was I supposed to know he was reaching for his wallet
after I asked for ID self-defense

We hold all of those born in the Abattoir

You hold us "hulk
"You hold us "charging like a bull
"You hold us "superpredators
"You hold our women who look like men, our men who look like
women
, and our women who look like we don't like men – thefreaksthecrazy
bitches

You hold these "truths" in a fist
around a standard-issue weapon
standard operating procedure
standard limited time desk duty
standard due process
standard no indictment
standard the one holding the gun and the one empty-handed are
equal
standard the one laughing, the one cashing
and the one decomposing

all "equal
" the "Daddy's home!" and the "Where's Daddy
?" equal

Lie, Berty

Lie Berty
and
just this
for all

Rimbaud is not Rambo

you laugh
we laugh
not the same
joke

White Woman Calls Police**

In 1955 in Money, Mississippi, a white woman accused 14-year-old Emmet Till of whistling at her. Shortly thereafter, his body was found beaten, mutilated, and weighted down so it would sink in a river. In 2008, the woman admits that she lied
White woman calls the police claiming that a 9-year-old Black boy groped her. Video later showed the boy's backpack bumped into her. October 2018, Brooklyn, New York
White woman, a mother on a college tour with her kid, calls police to complain that two Native American students "don't belong" there, in college, on the tour. May 2018, Fort Collins, Colorado
White woman college student calls police on Black woman college student who fell asleep in the common room of the dorm she lives in. May 2018, New Haven, Connecticut
White woman calls police to complain about Black people BBQing in a public park. September 2018, Oakland, California
White woman calls police to complain about a "threatening" Black woman – an assistant principal waiting for the bus to go to work. May 2018, Brooklyn, New York
White woman calls police on two Black men waiting for a friend to have a meeting in Starbucks. The men are arrested. May 2018, Philadelphia, Pennsylvania

White woman calls police on three Black women
leaving an air bnb; seven police cars show up and
police draw their guns on the women. May, 2018,
Rialto, California
White woman calls police on Black man moving into
his own apartment on the Upper West Side. April 2018,
New York, New York. The same thing happened to a
Black man who already lived in his apartment in Octo-
ber 2018, St. Louis, Missouri
White woman calls police on Black woman sheltering from
the rain in front of her building while she waited for a taxi.
July, 2018, Brooklyn, New York. In November 2013, a Black
woman who had gotten into a car accident walked to the
nearest house to ask for help. The white man who answered
the door shot and killed her, claiming that he thought she was
trying to break in. Dearborn Heights, Michigan
White woman calls police on 8-year-old Black girl selling water on
a hot day, complaining that she didn't have a license. June 2018, San
Francisco, California. White woman calls police on Black, 12-year-old
boy entrepreneur who, while mowing her neighbor's lawn, acciden-
tally mowed part of hers as well. June, 2018, Maple Heights, Ohio
White woman, upset that Black man has asked her to leash her dog
in a part of Central Park that requires it, threatens that she is going
to call police and tell them an African-American man is threatening
her. – and then does so. May 2020, New York City. White woman calls
police to report a Black man resting near his bicycle many feet away
on a public trail is "intimidating" her and preventing her from walking
by him. July 2020, Ottowa, Ontario. Woman calls police to complain
that there are thousands of Black people at Avenue L, that they don't
live there, and that she doesn't know what they're doing there. The
people were in line to vote. This threat was broadcast to some 9,000
people via local neighborhood watch sites. October 2020, Brooklyn,
New York

**Go to www.rosamondSking.black to see and contribute to a map documenting
this phenomenon.

what do you have
holstered? a badge
shield protective
forcefield membrane
called skin
? what is your matter
 translucent epidermis
 flat vowels nasal
accent? how is it working
for you
?

(in the wake of murders in Ocean Hill, Brooklyn and
Virginia Beach, Virginia

be clear
: bodies bleed beyond
the Abattoir
Elsewhere blood flows from children
between the bullies and the beaten
; blood floods in schools, movie
houses, cubicles
same color, same viscosity
. the difference? we don't get prayers
we don't even get thoughts

...

"I'm late to this party
"she repeated
distraught over
discovering the disasters
that will attack
her sons
.Her status
bred well
until her babies
.She couldn't
see the blood, thought
in Elsewhere, Abattoir
rules couldn't reach them
.Now
she arrives
at this "party
" prison for our sons
dark boys with Muslim names
– they were born for it – where
neither their faces nor
what we call them is considered
beautiful
– when they laugh, when
they dance
it is despite
not because

.

Better late than never
she dances with furious knowledge
we watch her
some sitting, some standing
doing the headnod
– we've heard this song before
when she's tired see
if she drinks the lead-heavy water
or if she slips out
to bring her boys pretty
colored kool-aid
oblivious to/o
us watching to see whether
someone who can leave
does anything
besides love her sons
and come late
again and

Becky wants to know

How old is your daughter
? Is she part Asian
? How did y o u
end up with a white
child? Becky tells you
the r(wh)ight way
to hold the baby
wants you to close the
window and while you
're over there, puh lease
pour her a drink, she's dead
tired had to chase
that infernal dog all over
her family's 200 acres only
to find her dead tired back
on the porch. Becky sees
you writing a poem wants
eighty per cent and her r(wh)ight
full name but inspiration
is not muse and the poem refuses
to record her given, sur, or proper

accessory after the fact

you are the bauble glinting murder into self-defense
you are the shrine of silence
you, on fleek, flicking fear on facebook
shackle bracelet
chokehold necklace

crimson-colored glasses

Palaces are always majestic
, impressive, and gauche

Palaces leave impressions
: gold slick with blood, fountains
pulsing it, jewels with smears
diminishing their clarity. Hold
onto the railing; you might slip

Double Valence

a 21st century
belly band torques around
the beast, distending it till
belly bust, our detained children
crawling out its twisted intestine
and jagged anus. we band belly
till we reclaim our children and
cleanse them with care

contra band

for a few hundred years our bodies
were contraband to our selves
not Iona, Queenie, Duke, Prince

now we own our bodies and nothing
else not where we live not how we
move not the phone we've paid for
every month for years our phone
is contraband, a phantom
gun. who owns our
children. not us. not the teacher
who makes her read the word
she's not allowed to say at home
our child who spends
childhood as a phantom
adult, getting grope-stopped by cops
looking for manhood confirmation
in twelve-year-old's panties
. contra band again
she is too
not owned by any
one band together against
for her and her own her ship
for this child, there is
no history older than Granny

Freedom

is awaiting the perfect conditions
is after the harvest
    next year's harvest
is coming, but
    this whole place needs to be cleaned first
will arrive with the rapture
requires just a little more _____
will not forget your sacrifice
remembers its own future
will be bestowed when they've learned how to behave
for some will have to remain pending
has been deferred until

Do not complete with colored pen
Do not fold or tear
Do not write below the line
Have your traditions ready for inspection
                                    or lack of may lead to expulsion

We will protect you by turning the army into the border patrol
We will protect you by turning the national guard into the police
We will protect you by turning the police into the paramilitary
We will protect you by attacking you in your homes

We will give you a receipt for your children

Here it is: this war never over
and others eased out carefully today
and today. A muffuletta of wars
: different flavors and textures, but all
the meat smoked, all the moldy cheese of death

.

It's meant to grind us
keep us chewing, face full
to gagging, they think retching
we won't ask who made this
why isn't there something else to eat

I can't breathe now
a double valence
, now everyone in the Abattoir
is Tyra Hunter except the
paramedics are not laughing
, except standing by and watching
the rest of us die is official policy
. Official or implied, the line's
the same – not worth
the energy of resuscitation, the cost
of ventilator or dialysis. The same
message: our *lifestyle* and
choices render us disposable, as
declared by systems whose choices
restrict our own, whose four hundred
year *lifestyle* rests comfortably on
our backs, sipping sugar–laced cocktails
from our skulls

Corona is in Queens

1
it's true
the virus does not discriminate
but Elsewhere is hard to find
these days, while the
sweaty, smelly Abattoir
bright with blood
is a gps beacon
.

so we're not exactly
#inthistogether
while Elsewhere #wfh, someone
has to make the meat, someone has to
package it, ring it up, deliver
–

already rife with Asthma
, Diabetes, Hypertension, Fibroids
, Endometriosis, Miscarriages
, Mental Illness

, , , ,

it's no wonder Corona is in Queens

2
some think it's fate
, luck, random
divine preordination
and some think it's design
:
more susceptible because
our overwork has been
essential and expendable
since 1619 and before
, and now, especially
;
never top of the list
for testing or admittance
or ventilator, not preferred
for insurance or relief
, only Corona recognizes us
crowns us Queens and Kings

.

The Curve Is Flattening

New hospitalizations: stable (hundreds
) New intubations: stable (hundreds
) New infections: slightly down (< one thousand
) Death rate: stable (hundreds
)

and we rejoice, curving
away from parks turned graveyards
some publicly sneaking a stoop
party, an unmasked picnic

unless yours is already dead
or alone, clawing at the new
ventilator without paralytics
to relax esophagus chafing

hastily trained tech running
to five others just like them and not

chaplain praying via phone
or post–it over forty others
just like you but not

Hopeyouandyours are well, means hope
oursarebetter, knowing thousands
will not see today's brilliant light
, clasp an ungloved hand, see
lips forming say-sos again
.

In a pandemic, some thousands have to
top the rollercoaster curve anticipating
not the rush and chortling against the bar
, sliding into safety, but the drop-off
into the nothing unknown

COVID19 Casualties 6 April 2020
: almost 75,000 reported deaths worldwide to date
, more than 4,700 recorded worldwide deaths yesterday
, more than 10,000 reported deaths in the USA to date
, 599 deaths in the USA recorded today, so far

. . .

COVID19 Casualties 14 July 2020
: more than half a million reported deaths worldwide
, more than 136,115 reported deaths in the USA so far

. . .

COVID19 Casualties 18 October 2020
: more than 1,114,715 reported deaths worldwide
, more than 219,680 reported deaths in the USA so far

. . .

COVID19 Casualties 6 January 2021
: more than 1,891,067 reported deaths worldwide so far
, a record 3,865 deaths, totalling 369,990 reported deaths in the USA
so far

. . .

Seven o'clock is just seven o'clock
in the Abattoir. Elsewhere People are
cheering; here, firefighters catcall
women with nowhere else to walk
since "bravest's" cars sidewalk-park
blaring flags and gun-toting bumper
stickers. Police menaced or dismissed us
before, dismiss and menace us now
… EMTs always thought we were
contaminated, and sirens just mean
someone's already dead
– Essential workers for us are
dollar store families rationing
tp, grocery teams hazarding
with minimum wage. So
no cheering at seven. Instead, at
nine, phone speakers and car radios
serenade the block with bass
. All songs same lyrics
: You still here? We still here

.

say it
: some living in
the Abattoir are
cannibals
drinking our own
since birth
chomping in
love in hate
indifference
: we'd offer
you a taste
but already
our blood is in
your sugar
cotton earbuds
dreams

There is
no over
: grief is
a wound
, then
it's a scar

Sunshine Sigh

know that we will and choose to spend our time before death living
, not passing our time until death dying

desire stronger than fear
more pulsing than threat
desire mek yu liquid flame
taller than
an hotter

desire lead yu by the nose hairs, promising
love and panic just there
just beyond   desire will drown yu
an as liquid becomes pummeling wave
flame still there   pulsating
crimson. sunrise
. citrus. dancing hot an hard
lovely an terrifying

stoop sun gazing

bottom on one step
hot stone pricking elbows

body leaning on body

a dark quiet

luminescent joy : the absence of attention
sunshine sigh of being left alone
lovely lackadaisicality on the stoop
reflecting caressing heat
still body : warm, pulsing, radiating

Have you seen life
? Did you lock hips
one hot cheek against
another? Did you spit looks
arguing the details
? Have you seen
  , or are you
still looking
>

Beautiful Things
I Saw Yesterday
:A Man Playing
Pattycake With
His Daughter. At
The Bus Stop
Mixing Live
On Turntable
Strapped to Her Chest
. Bowling Ball
With Milky White
Marbling That
Someone Had
Thrown Away

.

The World Itself
Broken, Pieces
Missing Yet
Not Rent Open
Not Completely

unfinished

we are safety

to each other

Letter to a ghost

 want to be
well. am sure
of it

thoroughly cleaned
  vessel. never
the same. spots
scratched, but clean

. some of us
get to live
, so some
of us are going
to live
...

sometimes
it is that
simple
: to survive

this blood-drenched crawling
wailing life is not possible
and neither is

blinking through scars
into a beaming sun without forgetting
  start with simple: living
is not possible
without life

No accident
, surviving

we want to live
. forgotten on the trudgy treadmill
between payday and pillow
through today's common despair

. do not be comforted. we
want to live. remember
by seeing small, 6 or 8
legs trudging or flying to
contentment. remember
by lingering with any
face divine. we want to
live. tilt yourself up; the same
vast is possible
before and behind our eyes

This poem knows your silence will not protect you
It sees you
Not knowing what to next

This is not the poem we wanted
The blank page in front of us is the ear of our grandchildren
Waiting
This was always going to be

About work

This poem
Cannot finish
Itself

Impossible

Lately we're doing as many
as six impossible things a day
: decent rooms for the unhoused
: unemployment benefits for gig workers
: health care for the uninsured
: waiving bail, depopulating prisons
: eviction and foreclosure moratoriums
: defunding the police
...
I'll tell you how imperfect it all is
in another poem, because now
is not Wonderland, or Neverland
, or Heaven, or Nirvana
...
or maybe now is, maybe we
always were, and we need to
open our eyes, work, believe
: imagine what we can do
tomorrow

ACKNOWLEDGEMENTS

Many thanks to those whose encouragement, work and resources helped to make this collection possible, including: laurie prendergast, Gabrielle Civil, Jen Bervin, and the Nightboat Team, especially Stephen Motika, Lindsey Bolt, and Caelan Nardone, and designer Astryd Design Inc.

Thanks to the editors and staff of these journals, anthologies, and blogs, in which some poems from *All the Rage* appeared, sometimes in earlier versions: *The Academy of American Poets' Poem-a-Day, Another Chicago Magazine, Aster(ix), Baest, The Cortland Review, The Feminist Wire, Harriet: The Poetry Foundation blog, Hyperallergic, The New Daughters of Africa, The North American Review,* and *Transition.*

Thanks to the curators and staff of the following venues and series, where significant portions of *All the Rage* were performed prior to publication: The Akilah Oliver Memorial Reading at Pratt Institute, The Brooklyn Ladies Text-Based Salon, The California Institute for the Arts, The Claremont Colleges, Dixon Place, Gibney Dance's Living Gallery Series, MetLiveArts at The Metropolitan Museum of Art (New York City), The National Black Writers Conference, Moe's Books, The South of Queer series at Brown University, The Segue Reading Series, The St. Mark's Poetry Project, The University of Illinois–Chicago, and Wooster College.

A grant from PSC–CUNY contributed to the production of this book.

The photographs that act as bookends are still images from "First Ladies," a work of solo performance art by Rosamond S. King performed at and commissioned by AfiriPerforma, the first African Performance Art Biennale. They were taken by Lotte Løvholm.

Rosamond S. King is a critical and creative writer and performer. She is also the author of *Rock | Salt | Stone* and *Island Bodies: Transgressive Sexualities in the Caribbean Imagination*. The goal of all of her work is to make people feel, wonder, and think, usually in that order.

www.rosamondSking.black

NIGHTBOAT BOOKS

Nightboat Books, a nonprofit organization, seeks to develop audiences for writers whose work resists convention and transcends boundaries. We publish books rich with poignancy, intelligence, and risk. Please visit nightboat.org to learn about our titles and how you can support our future publications.

The following individuals have supported the publication of this book. We thank them for their generosity and commitment to the mission of Nightboat Books:

Kazim Ali
Anonymous
Jean C. Ballantyne
Photios Giovanis
Amanda Greenberger
Elizabeth Motika
Benjamin Taylor
Peter Waldor
Jerrie Whitfield & Richard Motika

In addition, this book has been made possible, in part, by grants from the National Endowment for the Arts, the New York City Department of Cultural Affairs in partnership with the City Council, and the New York State Council on the Arts Literature Program.